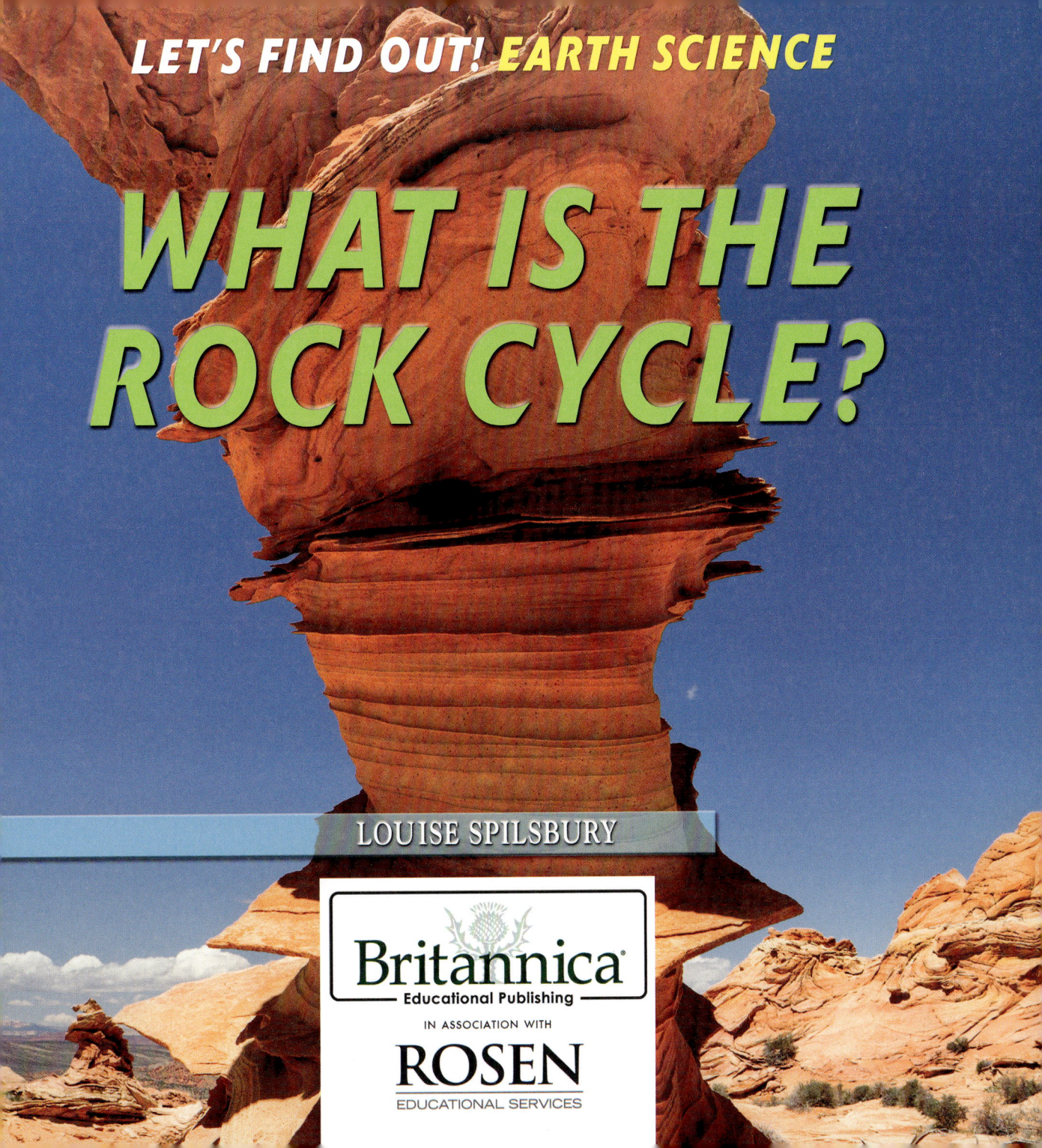

Published in 2014 by Britannica Educational Publishing (a trademark of Encyclopædia Britannica, Inc.) in association with The Rosen Publishing Group, Inc.
29 East 21st Street, New York, NY 10010

Copyright © 2014 by Encyclopædia Britannica, Inc. Britannica, Encyclopædia Britannica, and the Thistle logo are registered trademarks of Encyclopædia Britannica, Inc. All rights reserved.

Rosen Publishing materials copyright © 2014 The Rosen Publishing Group, Inc. All rights reserved.

Distributed exclusively by Rosen Publishing.
To see additional Britannica Educational Publishing titles, go to rosenpublishing.com

First Edition

Britannica Educational Publishing
J.E. Luebering: Director, Core Reference Group
Anthony L. Green: Editor, Compton's by Britannica

Rosen Publishing
Hope Lourie Killcoyne: Executive Editor
Nelson Sá: Art Director

Library of Congress Cataloging-in-Publication Data

Spilsbury, Louise.
What is the rock cycle?/Louise Spilsbury.
    p. cm. — (Let's find out: earth science)
Includes index.
ISBN 978-1-6227-5266-9 (library binding) — ISBN 978-1-6227-5269-0 (pbk.) — ISBN 978-1-6227-5270-6 (6-pack)
1. Petrology — Juvenile literature. 2. Geochemical cycles — Juvenile literature. I. Spilsbury, Louise. II. Title.
QE432.2 S65 2014
552–dc23

Manufactured in the United States of America

Photo credits
Cover: Shuterstock: M.Ellinger. Inside: Dreamstime: Cristiborda 24, Ctecu 7, Jasonjung 16, Jgrabert 27, Jkraft5 17, Johnmills12 13, Klikk 26, Liquidanbar 25, Metschurat 20, Milslav78 18, Mitchellb 21, Mrallen 14–15, Nicolegardner 28, Qwerty1983 19, Shayouk 29, Sprokop 23, Sugar0607 15, Tupatu76 22, Vlad3563 12, Vulkanette 10; Shutterstock: Bierchen 9t, Robert Crow 11, Givaga 5, M.Ellinger 1, 9r, Martin M303 4, Dr Ajay Kumar Singh 9l, Tr3gin 8, Webspark 6.

Contents

What Are Rocks?	4
Inside Earth	6
Recycling Rocks	8
Igneous Rocks	10
Crystals	12
Sedimentary Rocks	14
Fossils	16
Metamorphic Rocks	18
Shaping Rock	20
Weathering	22
Erosion	24
Soil	26
Rocks and People	28
Glossary	30
For More Information	31
Index	32

What are Rocks?

Rocks are the solid materials that make up most of Earth's surface. The surface is made of different types of rock. We see rocks around us every day. Rocks are in the walls of buildings, in the ground we walk on, and in the pebbles and cliffs at the beach. There are rocks under the sea and in the soil. Rocks make the landscapes we see around us.

The mighty Grand Canyon is made up of layers of different rock.

Granite is a hard rock made up of different colored minerals.

There is a huge variety of different rocks in the world. Rocks can be as small as a grain of sand or as big as a building. Some rocks are hard, but some are soft and crumbly. Rocks come in different colors, too, from pink, white, and silver to gray and black. Rocks are made from one or many minerals.

Minerals are the solid substances that make up rocks.

Inside Earth

Most minerals form deep inside Earth. Above the core, the center part of Earth, is a thick layer of extremely hot rock called the mantle. Earth's hard, rocky outer layer is called the crust. When rock deep in Earth's crust or the mantle melts, we call it magma. As magma flows upward, it cools. As it cools, different minerals inside it harden and become tiny, solid minerals that can form rocks.

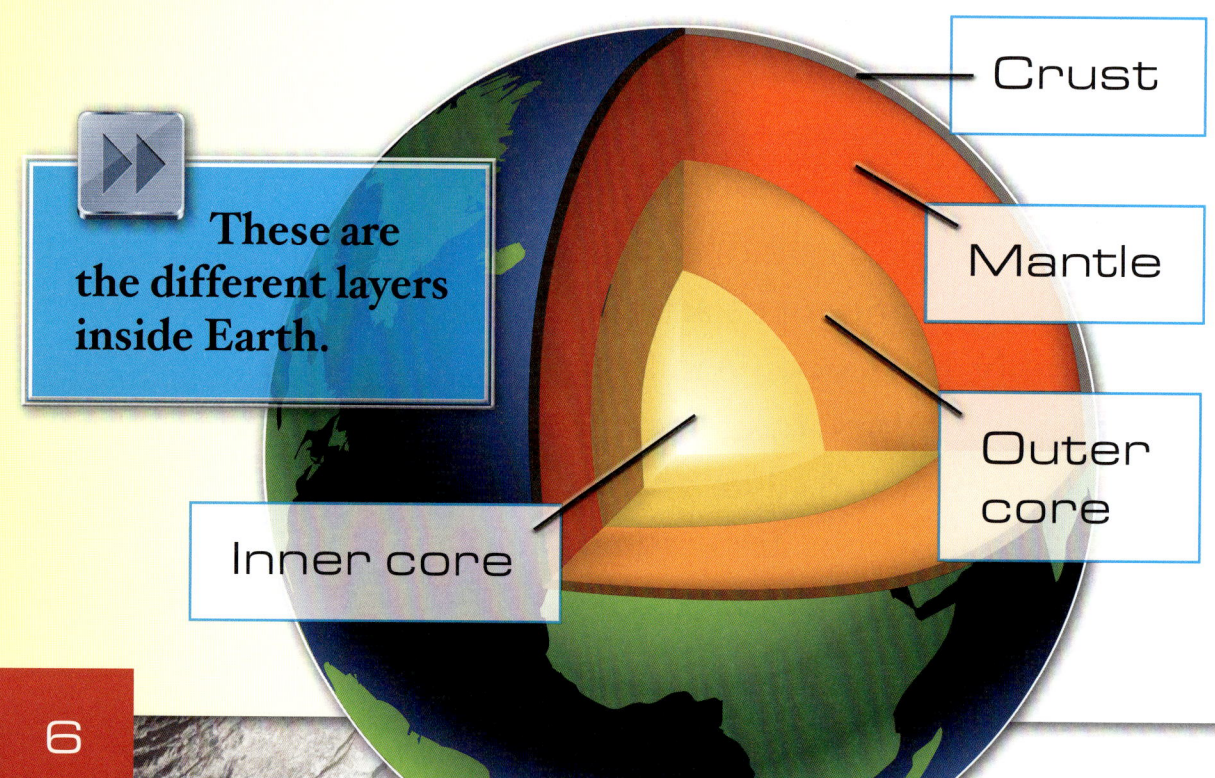

These are the different layers inside Earth.

Some minerals form when water gets under Earth's surface. Rain and seawater seep underground through cracks in the crust. Some of this water heats up if it reaches the hot mantle rock. Minerals in the very hot water mix with minerals from the mantle rock. When the water cools again, new minerals form.

A cave explorer catches water that drips down from the rock above him.

Think About It

When rocks heat up they change. How do we use heat to change things? How does heat change ice cream on a summer's day?

Recycling Rocks

Rocks do not stay the same. They are always changing because they are constantly being recycled. Rocks are formed, worn down, and then formed again in a process called the **rock cycle**. The rock cycle constantly recycles the minerals in Earth's crust.

The **rock cycle** is the process by which rocks of one kind change into rocks of another kind. The rock cycle takes many millions of years.

These many colorful rocks were formed during the rock cycle.

In the rock cycle, all rocks change slowly from one type to another, again and again.

Rocks can be divided into three main types: igneous, sedimentary, and metamorphic. The types of rock are defined by how they are formed in the rock cycle. Igneous and metamorphic rocks are the most common rock types in Earth's crust. Sedimentary rock is the most common rock type found at its surface.

Igneous Rocks

Igneous rocks form from hot magma that escapes from deep inside Earth. Earth's crust may seem solid and very strong, but there are places where it is weak. At these points, magma can sometimes build up and suddenly burst through the crust. This is what happens when volcanoes erupt.

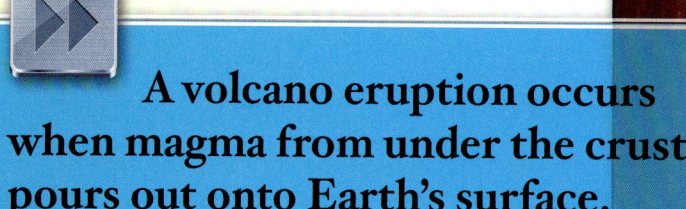

A volcano eruption occurs when magma from under the crust pours out onto Earth's surface.

THINK ABOUT IT

Some volcanoes erupt at the very bottom of an ocean. Could this explain how some islands form?

When hot lava cools, it becomes new rock.

When magma escapes onto Earth's surface, we call it lava. In the cool air above ground, the red-hot lava starts to quickly cool down. As it cools, it gets harder and becomes rock. The exact type of rock that forms depends on what minerals were in the magma, but two common igneous rocks are granite and basalt. Most of Earth's crust is made up of igneous rock.

Crystals

Crystals can form when the magma from inside Earth cools and hardens into rock. Crystals are made of minerals that have formed into shapes. These solid pieces of rock have flat sides and sharp, clear edges and corners. Minerals do not become crystal shapes if they form rock in spaces where there is not enough room to do so.

Amethyst is a very common quartz crystal.

The Giant's Causeway in Northern Ireland is made up of more than 40,000 basalt crystals.

THINK ABOUT IT

Why do you think crystals such as diamonds and sapphires are worth far more than quartz crystals, which make up most of the sand found on a beach?

Some crystals are very small, such as those that you find inside pieces of granite. Other crystals can be huge. Crystals are small if rock cools quickly. They are large if lava cools slowly into rock. Some crystals are dull and others are shiny or colorful.

Sedimentary Rocks

Sedimentary rock can be formed in several ways. Some are formed when rocks of any kind are worn away by wind, rain, and other elements. Through a process called erosion, tiny fragments of the original rock, along with dissolved minerals, are carried away to another site. Over time, millions of tiny pieces of sediment pile up on top of each other. Gradually, thick layers of sediment build up.

Sediment is a naturally formed material that is made of tiny pieces of rock, mud, or sand.

We can tell this is sedimentary rock because it is made up of different layers.

14

Limestone is sedimentary rock formed mainly from the tiny, broken remains of dead sea animals. That is why it is especially crumbly.

As the layers of sediment build up, the upper layers press down on the lower layers, squeezing the water out of them. The heavy weight of the upper layers presses the lower layers of mud, sand, and rock closer and closer together. Slowly, the pieces form new sedimentary rock.

Fossils

Sedimentary rocks often have fossils in them. Fossils are the remains of plants and animals that lived millions of years ago. Most fossils are of sea animals that had shells. When a sea animal died and sank to the sea floor, its body quickly rotted away. The shell that remained was gradually buried under many layers of sediment.

This fossil is of an ichthyosaur, an animal that swam in the oceans when dinosaurs roamed the land.

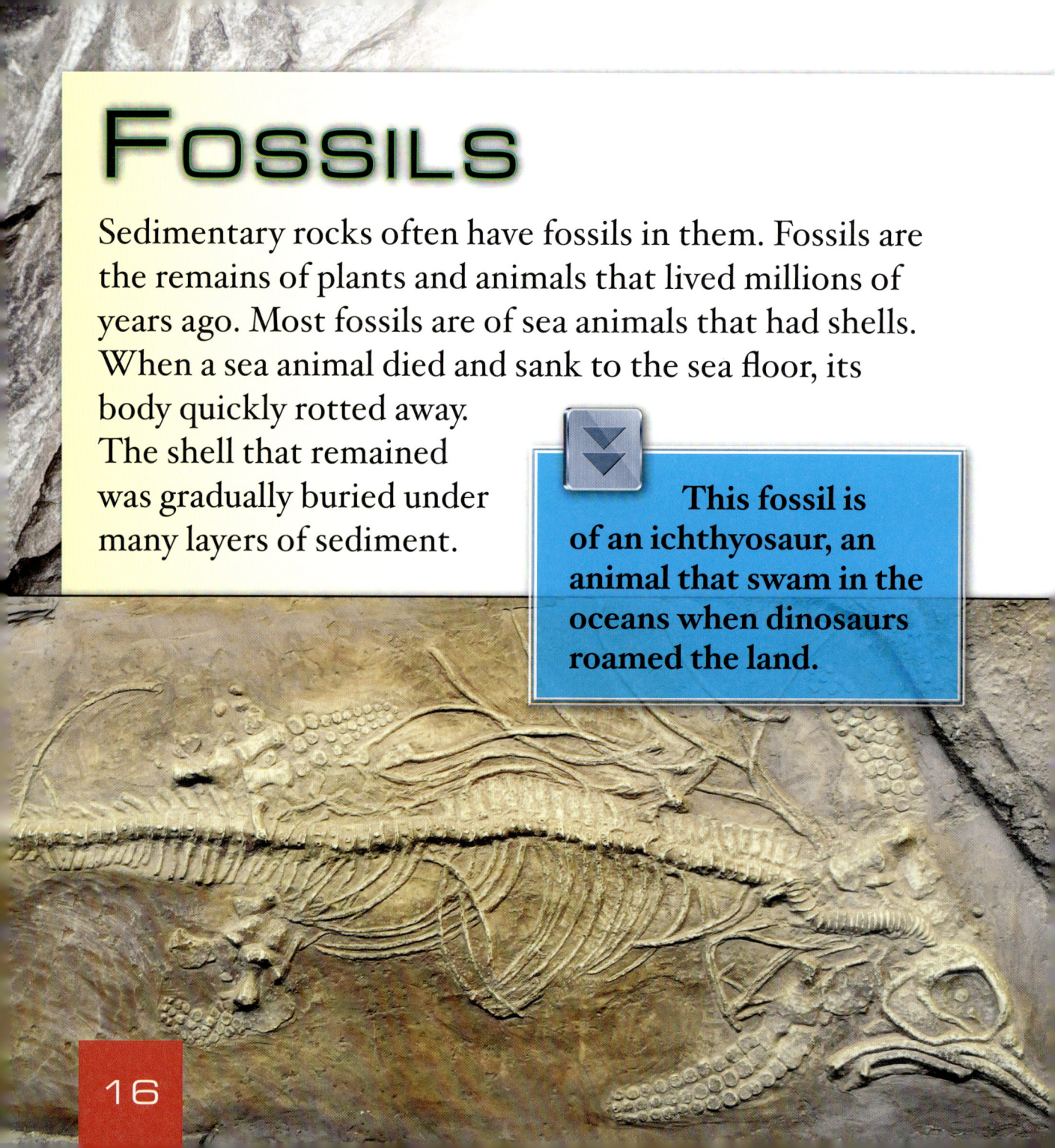

THINK ABOUT IT

Why do you think animals with shells were more likely to become fossils than other types of animals?

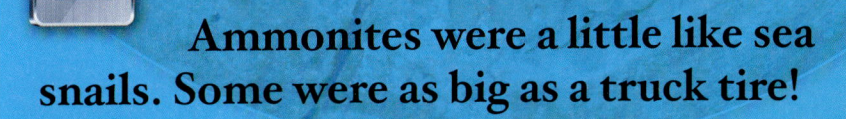

Ammonites were a little like sea snails. Some were as big as a truck tire!

Over hundreds of thousands of years, water carrying tiny pieces of sediment soaked into the shell. Gradually, minerals from the water replaced the minerals that made up the shell. The minerals turned into rock that was exactly the same shape as the shell, creating a fossil.

Other kinds of fossils are imprints on soft material that later hardened into rock, such as dinosaur footprints in mud.

Metamorphic Rocks

Metamorphic rock is formed when other rocks inside Earth are affected by great temperatures and pressures. There, it is extremely hot and the weight of the rock in the crust above presses down hard on the rock below. These conditions bake and break down minerals in the rock deep underground. When the minerals mix together again, they form new metamorphic rock. Metamorphic rock can be formed from sedimentary or igneous rocks.

Marble is a metamorphic rock.

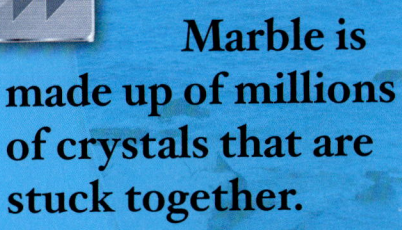

Marble is made up of millions of crystals that are stuck together.

Metamorphic rock often forms in places where large sections of Earth's crust called plates push against each other. The rock can also form where magma is forced through existing rocks, heating them and increasing pressure.

Think About It

Metamorphic rocks are not made by melting rocks. How does this differ from the way that igneous rocks are made?

19

Shaping Rock

Some metamorphic rocks have wiggly lines running through them. They are created when the crust moves slightly over the hot, bubbling mantle inside Earth. As the crust moves, the extreme heat and **pressure** from the rocks above twists and shapes metamorphic rock as it forms.

Pressure is a weight that pushes down heavily on something.

Gneiss is metamorphic rock with colored minerals twisted into bands by great pressure.

Slate is a metamorphic rock formed by extreme pressure underground. It is created by minerals that once made up a sedimentary rock called shale. The minerals that form slate are quite thin and flaky. Layers of slate break off easily into thin slabs. This is what makes slate such a useful material for making roof tiles used for building.

Slate is used for roof tiles because it is tough and strong, and also because it splits easily into tiles.

Weathering

Even the hardest, toughest rocks do not last forever. All rocks on Earth's surface are affected by weathering. They are worn away and broken down into smaller pieces by the action of wind, water, and ice. When water gets into gaps in a rock and freezes into ice, it takes up more space. This makes the rock crack and break.

On cold mountaintops, ice can make rock crack and break off.

▶▶ Wind-blown sand can rub and grind away rock into arches and other shapes.

On the coast, waves crash against the rocks and toss other rocks and stones at them. This breaks up rock and wears it away. Rain can contain substances that **dissolve** rock and break it up. In sandy places, wind whips up many tiny pieces of sand and smashes them against rock. This action wears away the rock.

Dissolving is when a solid breaks down into a liquid.

23

Erosion

Erosion is the movement of small pieces of rock broken up by weathering. Water, wind, and other natural forces cause rocks and earth to wear away, or erode. Erosion happens in different ways. Some broken pieces of rock simply drop to the ground, and slip or roll down slopes. Others are carried off by rivers and streams. Wind picks up and carries small grains of sand. Glaciers are slow-moving rivers of ice, and they can shift or erode even big pieces of stone.

Wind eroded pieces from this rock to leave behind this amazing shape.

The tiny pieces of rock do not carry on moving. Eventually, the wind stops blowing, rivers flow into the sea, and glaciers melt. Then they drop the pieces of rock they were carrying. This process is called deposition. These tiny pieces of sand, mud, and pebbles gradually become buried and transformed into sedimentary rock.

> **COMPARE AND CONTRAST**
> What are the similarities and differences between weathering, erosion, and deposition?

Water can carry tiny pieces of rock a long way, until it finally drops them.

25

Soil

Some of the main ingredients of soil are the tiny pieces of rock and sand formed by weathering and erosion. This is not yet soil. First, plants start to grow among the bits of rock. This helps to open up spaces between the pieces. Then, water, air, and animal or plant remains pass through the spaces. All these things combine to form what we call soil.

Soil builds up on top of a layer of hard rock.

Think About It

Why do people try to stop the erosion of top layers of soil, for example by building walls around a sloping field?

⏩ **Most plants need soil to grow and we need plants to provide us with food.**

Soil is an important part of the rock cycle. Plants grow in the top layer of soil. The waste in this layer contains nutrients. Without plants to eat or to feed the animals that provide people with meat, humans would not survive.

Soil forms slowly. A layer of soil that is 1 inch (2.5 cm) thick may take 500 to 1,000 years to form. For this reason it is important to protect soil from erosion.

Rocks and People

The rock cycle provides us with soil in which to grow food, but rocks are used in other ways, too. People cut rocks such as granite to make building materials. They use quartz from sand to make glass. Concrete is made from tiny pieces of rock and sand mixed with cement. Rock is mixed with tar to make the surface of streets.

People use rocks to make the buildings, houses, and streets all around us.

THINK ABOUT IT
We are using up Earth's supply of oil and gas very quickly. Why will there be no more when the supplies run out?

Without the rock cycle, there would be no fuel!

The gas in our cars and most of the electricity we use to power machines such as computers comes from fossil fuels. Coal, oil, and natural gas are fossil fuels. They formed from ancient plant and animal remains. The heavy weight of all the rock forming above the remains helped to turn them into the fuels we rely on today.

Glossary

basalt A very hard type of igneous rock.
core The center of Earth.
crust The hard, rocky layer on the surface of Earth.
crystals Solid pieces of rock with flat sides and sharp, clear edges and corners.
deposition The act of depositing or dropping something.
erosion The movement of small pieces of rock broken up by weathering.
fossil fuels Coal, oil, and natural gas formed from the remains of living things that died millions of years ago.
freezes When water turns into ice.
glaciers Slow-moving rivers of ice.
granite A very hard type of igneous rock.
igneous rocks Rocks formed from magma at or below the surface of Earth.
landscapes Natural features found on Earth's surface.
lava The name for magma when it emerges above Earth's surface.
magma Melted rock usually found beneath Earth's crust.
mantle The very deep layer of hot rock beneath Earth's crust and above the core.
metamorphic rocks Rocks that changed from their original form by heat and/or pressure.
nutrients The substances that feed living things and help them live and grow.
quartz A type of crystal.
recycled Having taken something old and refreshed or changed it into something new.
sedimentary rocks Rocks made when tiny pieces of rock or shells are changed by heat and pressure into rock.
volcanoes Openings in Earth's surface where magma escapes from underground.
weathering The wearing away and breaking down of rock into smaller pieces by the action of wind, water, and ice.

For More Information

Books

Harman, Rebecca. *Rock Cycles: Formation, Properties, and Erosion* (Earth's Processes). North Mankato, MN: Heinemann, 2006.

Hoffman, Steven M. *Weathering and Erosion: Wearing Down Rocks* (Rock It!). New York, NY: PowerKids Press, 2011.

Morgan, Sally. *Rocks* (Earth Cycles). Mankato, MN: Smart Apple Media, 2012.

Riley, Joelle. *Examining Erosion* (Searchlight Books: Do You Dig Earth Science?). Minneapolis, MN: Lerner Classroom, 2013.

Weidner Zoehfeld, Kathleen. *Rocks and Minerals* (National Geographic Readers). Washington, D.C.: National Geographic Children's Books, 2012.

Websites

Due to the changing nature of Internet links, Rosen Publishing has developed an online list of Websites related to the subject of this book. This site is updated regularly. Please use this link to access the list:

http://www.rosenlinks.com/lfo/rock

Index

amethyst 12
ammonites 17
animals 15, 16, 17, 26, 27, 29
arches 23

basalt 11, 13
beach 4, 13
building materials 28
buildings 4, 21, 28

cave explorers 7
cement 28
cliffs 4
core 6
crust 6, 7, 8, 9, 10, 11, 18, 19, 20
crystals 12–13, 19

deposition 25
diamonds 13
dinosaurs 16, 17

Earth 4, 6–7, 8, 9, 10, 11, 12, 18, 19, 20, 22, 29
erosion 14, 24–25, 26, 27

fossil fuels 29
fossils 16–17

Giant's Causeway 13
glaciers 24, 25
glass 28
gneiss 20
Grand Canyon 4
granite 5, 11, 13, 28

ice 22, 24
ichthyosaur 16
igneous rocks 9, 10–11, 18, 19

landscapes 4
lava 11, 13
limestone 15

magma 6, 10, 11, 12, 19
mantle 6, 7, 20
marble 18, 19
metamorphic rocks 9, 18–19, 20, 21
minerals 5, 6, 7, 8, 11, 12, 14, 17, 18, 20, 21
mud 14, 15, 17, 25

nutrients 27

ocean 11, 16

pebbles 4, 25
plants 16, 26, 27, 29

quartz 12, 13, 28

rain 7, 14, 23
recycling 8–9
rivers 24, 25

sapphires 13
sea 4, 16, 25
    sea animals 15, 16, 17
seawater 7
sediment 14, 15, 16, 17
sedimentary rocks 9, 14–15, 16, 18, 21, 25
shale 21
shells 16, 17
slate 21
soil 4, 26–27, 28

volcanoes 10, 11

water 7, 15, 17, 22, 24, 25, 26
waves 23
weathering 22–23, 24, 25, 26
wind 14, 22, 23, 24, 25